Losing It

Distributed by: Small Press Distribution (SPD), 1341 Seventh Street, Berkeley CA 94710;
American News Company, LLC., 1955 Lake Park Drive, Suite 400, Smyrna, GA 30080;
Media Solutions, 9632 Madison Blvd, Madison, AL 35758.

Available also from Box Turtle Press.
184 Franklin Street
New York, New York 10013
212.219.9278; mudfishmag@aol.com
www.mudfish.org

ISBN: 978-1-893654-25-9

Front Cover Image: "Back View," 1977, Philip Guston, oil on canvas, 69" h x 94" w
© The Estate of Philip Guston, Courtesy Hauser & Wirth. The painting is also reproduced by
the permission of the San Francisco Museum of Modern Art. Back Cover: Painting details.

Book design: Anne Lawrence
Typeset in Futura Book

Copyright © 2021 Richard J. Fein
Publisher: Box Turtle Press

MUDFISH INDIVIDUAL POET SERIES #15

Losing It

Richard J. Fein

Box Turtle Press/Attitude Art, Inc.
184 Franklin Street, New York, New York 10013

Also By Richard J. Fein:

Poetry

Selected Poems of Yankev Glatshteyn (translations)
Kafka's Ear
At the Turkish Bath
To Move into the House
Ice like Morsels
I Think of Our Lives: New and Selected Poems
Mother Tongue
Reversion
With Everything We've Got (translations)
B'KLYN
My Hands Remember
Not a Separate Surge: New and Selected Poems
The Full Pomegranate: Poems of Avrom Sutzkever (translations)
Whitman/Vitman

Prose

Robert Lowell
The Dance of Leah
Yiddish Genesis

For Marsi and Miriam

"This neither is its courage nor its choice,
  But its necessity in being old."

                    Wordsworth, "The Small Celandine"

CONTENTS

V

KOL NIDRE

—Moyshe-Leyb Halpern

The old clown from Karakhamba
used to shred onion into his coffee.
"I am sad," I say to myself,
with the melody of "Kol Nidre" in the dark.

How oddly his red eyes
blinked over the clay cup;
with a plain wooden spoon
he ate the onion with his coffee.

And seven days of autumn rain on the window
won't remind you of death
as want does, moaning drawing out
its moaning in each sip.

"I will go where my forefathers have gone,"
the open mouth said to the wooden spoon;
"my wife, Baleyke, is already there.
I will go where my forefathers have gone."

The pieces of onion in the spoon
looked like broken pearls;
yet they also looked like tobacco-yellowed
thin fingers playing a dulcimer.

In a dress of many yards of cloth
Baleyke danced before her groom.

Why are you crying, clown from Karakhamba,
this is only my Kol-Nidre-melody.

The clay coffee cup is warm,
like my heart, which was born blind;
and the onion, that shredded onion,
is as bitter as my sadness in the dark.

I

FAREWELL, JACOBO AND PAULINA

Unsidewalked muddy streets of your village emerged from your burly speech,
as did wooden walls housing prayer, ritual, chant, swaying bodies,
those walls painted with the floating gait of an antelope, with doves
hovering over a zodiac, with two rampant lions bearing notched tablets,
with flaming antlers without a body, like twigs on fire.
All this you pictured around the kitchen table while each of you pointed
an index finger upward as if those images survived steerage
and resided in our cramped apartment, there, *there*,
within the receding projections of the cornice bordering wall and ceiling,
your old eyes and my child eyes peering at the convexed molding,
you remembering what was once first-hand to you, once as immediate to you
as bulbous green glass on power lines or embossed manhole covers are to me.
Farewell, Jacobo and Paulina, your memories, tinged by another century,
were marooned on our sepia-Europe photos, while your old-country gab
was like a drawer of coins and paper money that have outlived their currency,
yet the two of you stare at me in your inlaid oval frames
as if a transparent embalmment lies between your faces and the glass.
O, Jacobo and Paulina, your very bodies were creased with accents
and strains you brought to me over versts, steppe, taiga, your speech
near the stove's pilot light that whooshed flames to outlying jets.

IN CENTRAL PARK

—Moyshe-Leyb Halpern

Whose fault is it that your tree is unseen,
garden in snow, my garden in snow.
Whose fault is it that your tree is unseen,
that a woman goes walking in you
and her breasts rise and tremble
like a ship on agitated waves and foam,
a ship on the ocean with two pirates
yelping, they are two pirates—
garden in snow, my garden in snow.

Whose fault is it that there is no deer,
garden in snow, my garden in snow.
Whose fault is it that there is no deer,
that a priest who has to be as pious as a child
runs after his hat in the wind
and shouts after it "hey" and "ho" and "hallo"!
And the hat in its desperate swirl
doesn't hear him, in its desperate swirl—
garden in snow, my garden in snow.

Whose fault is it that I'm a stranger to you,
garden in snow, my garden in snow.
Whose fault is it that I'm a stranger to you,
that I still wear my scarf and my hat,
the likes of which nobody else in this whole country owns,
I who have the kind of beard your wind parts,
the way a woman parts straw while looking for an egg
for her sick child, looking for an egg from a hen—
garden in snow, my garden in snow.

ONLY NOW

"What did you know of them?" I ask myself,
and immediately my heart feels vacant
and then turns heavy, and then there is a shudder
in my breast—my visceral voucher
that I never really saw them for themselves,
outside of my own existence, my own focus.
For even the album's sepia, featheredged photos—
of them on the sand in their strapped beachwear,
or of them waving animatedly from the rumble seat,
or of them posing in hats, suit and dress
at the old pump my father used to prime,
and that later I used to prime—
were just dated pictures of them pre-me.
Their early, wistful years—young Abraham dreaming
of owning his own shoestore, young Esther planning
on going to normal school—seem like a vacant space
in a photograph album, a measure of black, corner-
framed by four paper arrowheads from which
a picture has fallen out and disappeared—
and suddenly, as I gaze at other pictures in the album,
the whole family history that produced me ebbs
into a realm where bodies are specters of themselves.

WHEN I WAS ABOUT TEN

I don't remember the movie exactly—
Dancing to Rio or starring Dolores del Rio?—
but my mother and I were on the way
to the movies one Sunday afternoon,
something we rarely did together alone,
and as we turned the corner and passed
Brownstein's butcher shop I saw the gouged
movie theater placard hanging on tenterhooks,
which during the week pierced meats
and chickens, the silver tips now thrusting
through what's playing and it suddenly
struck me that the name of the movie
which I was reading would transform into
the movie itself on the screen, in the dark,
and meanwhile on the window was *kosher*,
whose lettering was at one and the same time
both Hebrew and Yiddish and underneath it
was the word *kosher* in block English lettering,
all the characters in both versions—
one right to left and one left to right—
painted in red and outlined in white,
the brush strokes so uneven that sometimes
glass streaked through like a third color,
and then I stared past that huge window
and saw sawdust all over the floor, just as
I'd see in Berman's butcher shop, and Taub's,
which we'd also pass on the way to the movies,
and come Monday all those floors would be
swept clean, naked chickens—goose-pimply,
yellowy bluish, with stretched necks, limp combs—
hanging there again on the rows of silver hooks.

STICKBALL

I was never so inventive as I was at ten or eleven when
I retrieved an old broom from where it leaned among the garbage cans
along the curb, left for pickup, poking above the uneasy lids,
the broom no longer able to sweep the entranceway, the stoop, the pavement.
I took it with me down to the basement where I snatched
the super's long saw with the finger grips on the wooden handle
and I sawed off the bottom of the broom, several inches above
the wiry collar that clamped a hard knob of straw that then shouldered
down into the sweeping-bristles themselves, those fibers no longer
held in place by three rings of nodular scarlet thread, saggy now,
the end of those bristles worn down to a dirty, rough, aslant edge
as if the straw, so clumped and warped, had been hacked by a machete.
After I made my bat, I returned the leftover to the garbage,
that remnant broom idling on the unsettled garbage can cover,
a kind of amputee, with its few inches of handle, its newly made stub
a shining grainy testimonial to its uselessness, although that wiry metal collar
was still holding, still clamping, its ridged rings reminding me
of the screw threads inside a socket gripping and gripping a bulb
           until it lights up,
and then that stump-broom, varied fetish, suddenly turned into
a huge worn whisk broom a Gargantua might have used for brushing a suit.

I the bat-maker practiced my new swings as if I were really at bat—
I the new-born slugger smashing the ball with the bat I just made,
grasping it at or near or slightly up from the edge, testing
my various grips in the swings, the tips of my fingers
gingerly gauging the muscle of the bat where the wood would meet the ball.
In real games I got hits, scored runs, or fouled the ball off,
           or missed the pitch altogether.
I have athletic memories of the difference in the bounce between

the spaldeen and the tennis ball and the difference in their textures
and the way my fingers could impinge on the spaldeen but not on the tennis ball,
those differences affecting my batting and my catching and my pitching
          and the very sound of the ball on the bat,
the expectancies of skip and bounce and roll depending on the type of ball
          we threw, hit and caught on any given day,
any given day when I took my swings at home plate with that bat I made,
and I have memories of the stone-drawn bases and the fish-skeleton
          scoreboard we scratched on the street.

QUOTATION POEM

I read a passage by Marcel Proust
and turned it into lines of a poem,
folded it up and put it in my wallet,
near my United Health Care Card. Sometimes
I see it when fishing for a card or license:
"Those who are haunted by their confused
remembrance of truths they have never known
are the men who are gifted. ...Talent
is like a kind of memory, which in the end
enables them to call back this confused music,
to hear it distinctly, to write it down,
to reproduce it, to sing it." I am both puzzled
and touched by this passage I carry around, and
sometimes after I write a poem I think it's happened.

ELEMENTARY SCHOOL

Upper and lower cases of penmanship-regimen on ruled cardboard
tacked to corkboard above the blackboard and under the jutting American flag
always meet us in any classroom we walk into, the trim letters
informing me at how inept I am at shaping my *characters, befuddling* my peas
        and cues and jeez.
These pre-words and primal sonants signal my *unsatisfactory demeanor.*
These curls and bends and flecks and bulges and bows and curves and gulfs,
        righteous in their accusing neatness,
spell a cursive skill that can never be mine, that I will never be worthy of,
especially when I am *summoned* to the blackboard to write under the guardianship
of flag and penmanship, their perfections chastely looking down on me,
on my scrawly longhand and calcified sixth finger that screaks on the slate
and has a habit of breaking off into two pieces, the top part thunking
        into the wooden trough.
That fret-saw alphabet not only insinuates complaints about my writing
but also evokes my fear of my speech *impediment,* which I just might prevent
if I insert breaths or uhs or elongations or dummy articles or fusing-syllables,
though even then sounds might stick in my throat, knot in my tongue,
        quiver on my lips—shame embodied—
each time it's my turn for *recitation, conjugation, elocution.*
No matter how quick I am at Friday's History Quiz or how adept at locating
rivers, mountains, borders, capitals, deserts, inlets in Geography class,
that pristine alphabet remains a rebuke to me, a haven I cannot reach.
All I can do in the face of that order, placement, precision, neatness,
duplicated exactness of spacing, aligned perfection, consistent width
is *botch* things up as if the letters were daring me to try and use them,
lined up there like those standoffish straight-A girls twelve years old
and bound for the *Honor Roll* in their pleated skirts and white middy blouses.
Those out-of-reach letterings are a perfectly ordered dominance promoting
        proper usage, a cold splendor not unlike
the spikes on each of the forty-eight stars in their blue field.

Yet those letters could loosen up, jostle and join in combinations,
like the blue run of Dodgers across white jerseys, athletic
flow spelling out a charmed name across the chests, blue-looped name
with a decorative capital D and final s gliding into a widening
underline flourish whose design I only later came to know as *paraph*.

AMERICAN HERITAGE DICTIONARY OF THE ENGLISH LANGUAGE

I duct-taped your front cover to your spine and back cover
and held you upright, firmly gripping you as I gingerly
tapped you up and down on the stand, encouraging
everything to be in place, all of you holding together,
and in the process I found myself staring at the top
of your incurvate pages so compressed and swirled inward
they looked like emigrant-waves from a Japanese print,
some even having made their way into the gulf between
the binding and the spine when the front cover
was hanging askew, like the injured wing of a bird,
my makeshift adhesion now holding you together again
after fifty years of my opening you, fingering you,
the tips of my fingers expectantly moving down you,
or across you, seeking spellings, syllables, sounds,
definitions, origins, earlier or secondary meanings,
usage sometimes marked "slang," "regional," "archaic,"
those fingers unraveling your pages to get to my word, as
I even love getting lost or going astray along my way
and landing on another word of yours, where I linger,
touching and mouthing that word too, delightfully
diverted from where I was originally headed, coming
away with something new, a meaning, a spelling, a sound,
but now the early pages clump up and the outside columns
of your a's wear away, rip, tear off, some pages so curved
inward they look like roll-your-owns or hollow wafers, pages
dog-eared as far as the t's, corners so folded over
I have to peel back the flap to get the full entry.
But I don't have the heart to throw you out because you

pulse in my heart and I still love to hold you, sometimes
carrying you over to spread you out under even more light.
I still love touching you, once again looking up a word,
as I did this morning, thumbing for *spavined and entropy* again—
oh, both of you, words that I love to speak, taste and see
even as I lose your meanings in the slippage of my memory.
Wordpages, you'll last a little longer. We've been together so long,
even though we must admit you don't have an entry for that hyphenated act
I did to keep you together. It will never verb into you, alas.
But when you do fall apart, my mending insufficient—more
and more of the pages turning inward, creasing, becoming parchmenty,
difficult to unravel, more and more tearing off at the edges, it getting
trickier to fold back the corners and reveal what's hidden—oh,
then, my treasure, my garner—let your words, my words—
my words, your words—crumble in my hands and fingers, usage going,
all the gold letters on your terraced alphabet tabs having
flaked away, leaving behind them vacant, sallow half-moons.

A WORD IN THE MOUTH

—Yankev Glatshteyn

What do you own that's really yours?
A word in the mouth.
Take the meaning and conceal it.
Come to the world in a crown of dusk.
Hold out your hand and beg.

Events fall like hail on a frightened world.
Save yourself, disguised as a shadow.
Diminished and null, stricken and weary.
Let the tower of your poem be covered by snow.

Banish your heir.
Reject your last *kaddish*.
Those loins that pushed you into life—destroyed.
Your language in the mouth of an aged parrot.
The flash of your eye will also soon die out.

Across from you on a bench in the wretched poorhouse
the God of your fathers sits, worn out and sick.
The mighty, magnificent, ever-present God
is also like a mocked, rejected beggar.

Don't condemn Him.
Seek the virtues in a ruined Jew.
Like a night chorus in spiderwebbed sleep,
the remnants of a last generation dream.
Be like a Levi-Yitzkhok to Him.

1946

PRAYER
—Yankev Glatshteyn

The old beautiful Yiddish translation
missends the words of my prayer to You.
My praise incenses the air with a godly fragrance.
I pray to You from a mute book of prayers,
my sad God.

The least flower gives You more satisfaction
than the whole six-day creation.
The inertia of our destructive life
is the least of Your concerns.
You bestow on us thousands of years from the mountain
and hide Your face from us.
The walls of our houses drip with stupidity.

We can't even know the ABC's of holiness.
How many thousands of lives does one need
before one can imagine sitting at Your feet?
I pray to You from a mute book of prayers,
my sad God.

You are not fearsome. You are not angry.
You are only far from us
when we desecrate the moments of our life.
No matter how many flashes of eternity we have to smell,
our nostrils can't get rid of the stink of the *Khorbm*.
I pray to You from a mute book of prayers,
my sad God.

Khorbm: Holocaust.

II

INTERNAL RHYME

(for Melissa Green)

After the reading to save your house
you enter the reception wearing long
green gloves sheathing your forearms,
like Rita Hayworth in *Gilda*, who craftily
peeled them off to "put the blame
on Mame, boys, put the blame on Mame."
I was just a boy and it was the way
she sang and shed that got to me, her gloves,
like yours, with braided design, each
trimmed at the opening, where the exposure begins.

IRVING

The glaring clocks on the Con Ed tower—their gothic hands
pointing upwards or downwards or sideways or slantways, the minute
sometimes mounted on the hour before they made space between them—
stared down at me, as if on a boding Hopper building, as we walked along 14th Street
before we made our left turn onto Irving Place, heading toward
Washington Irving High School and the chamber music concerts
we would go to on a regular basis (special price for students);
and just after we turned we passed the Irving Place Theater
(which I later learned used to be a Yiddish theater)
with its steady program of Soviet films and all those modern classics
        I loved, *Grand Illusion* most of all.
Just two more blocks further up Irving Place was the National
        Hospital for Speech Disorders,
which I attended when I was in high school and wrote off as another cure
        that never worked,
and decades later I went to the end of Irving Place to visit Ruth Rubin
        and to hear her sing Yiddish folk songs,
but always during our walk it was the glowing faces of the skyscraper-herm
        that gripped me—
those outsize numerals, the eight black arrows marking time above
        the dark shaft of the Con Ed.
And then after the concert, while you guided me through the music
        we had just heard,
we headed back to your tiny apartment in the Village, a few doors down
        from the New School,
where we made love, four feet from your hot plate, in our tight joy,
and slowly our faults, our sated reciprocations, our mutual withdrawals,
fed off of each other until we couldn't stomach it anymore,
and then my lifetime-later move to Irving Street, where I live now and sit and write,
going back, re-tracing, re-seeing the tower clocks glowering down at me
on our way to the chamber music played by quartets whose place names
(like Budapest) always intimated something other than themselves.

ON WEST 12TH

You wrenched your mole colored dress down over your hidden head,
your bra, panties disappearing as you tugged on the dress,
your breasts garment-compacted as the creases sorted out, the dress
collar-settled, hemline-evened, zipper-zippered, waist-snugged,
and I watched you getting yourself ready for the office,
in walking distance, down on Sixth, where the Village ended.
Watching you, I closed my Henry James I was reading for class,
my index finger in the book, my thumb on the cover,
you turning from lover to employee, from roamer to pedestrian.
Watching you piece by piece putting yourself back together
after night's disarray, did I catch this was a special moment,
showing me we failed to enter the bareness we needed most of all?
And then, as if I could re-make this old re-run, I put my book down,
lose my place, get up from the chair, reach towards you
and work your dress back up until your head is a huge bulge
again under that mole colored fabric and reappears, disheveled,
and you pull my sweater over my head, a hidden bulge, then reappearing,
and there we are, face to face, fingers reciprocating, with further
        undressing to go.

WEST 75TH

"Why are you crying?"
"Oh... it's nothing,"
your head turned.
I didn't understand.
I remember the pink nodule
in the corner of your eye,
a birthmark bordering your lip.
"Oh... it's nothing."
Our faces close,
that was the moment
for me to reach further,
for you to respond further,
for us to further talk.
But I rolled off of you
and the moment fell away.
And nothing happened.

FACE TO FACE

Sitting,
thigh over thigh, thigh under thigh,
thighs straining to stay in place,
her hands seizing his shoulders,
so she could stay in place,
and he could stay in place,
his hands cupping.
Groin to groin,
they work at staying joined,
desire jostling between their bodies.

SHE REMEMBERS ACROSS THE YEARS

After he slid out of me and peeled off from the gummy sweat, listing
     toward the edge of the bed,
I saw filmy red smears on the shaft, furrow and head,
its very tip a pore in blood, and it suddenly came to me, as his body
     jostled off me,
that our lovemaking descended to a disobedience that brought us closer,
making for a kind of covenant between us, so that even without my
     confessing all to him
he had been touched by all of me, his dear pud so stained
by my fluid slough it was now glossed by my insides
as if his pumping and coming and my ooze and slaver
made a grease so primal we had become two creatures so effuse
that all would readily flow and we would speak of what I had done and why
and speak of what he had done, or not done, and why,
and we would reach forgiveness as we sensed nothing could block us now
     from opening up together
and distrust and fear and shame and withdrawal would all dissolve—
our chemistries so mixed that surely, now, forgiveness would flow
     from that, and

I watch him: he reaches for the handy tissue he flicks from the
     slit of the box

THEIR FAULTS MESHED…

Their faults meshed even more than their bodies did, psyche-selection—
his desire to be exempt from life, as he now sees himself back then,
bound to fail by his very coming to love her within his holding back,
and her desire to be protected, as she now sees herself back then,
bound to fail by her very coming to love him within her siege of shame,
each one's love harboring a defect that educed the love and defect in the other,
and so in their very love they were made to hurt each other,
talking though not talking, pleasures prompting evasions, touch out of touch.

*   *   *   *

In old age I conjure them up together (how much time is left now anyway?)
and he would lie in her lap and cry and she would lie in his and cry,
and they would take turns as a sitter soothing the other's head,
or they would hold each other, a tremor-embrace of two creatures
in tears, silence, groans, followed by admission-talk, owning up,
and then their doing the most ordinary things one does in life.
There's no making up for what they did or didn't—one want
bringing out the other want—that's what landed in their laps.

TO A WOMAN REMEMBERED

I will die, just as you will—you and I
unknown to ourselves and to each other,
when ears can't hear or tongue make sounds.
Even a young poet who longs to lay a girl
as I did you will in time lack everything.
All shapes will disappear from my mind,
even the ghost of you lingering there,
your voice coming down the stairwell,
"Is that you, Richard?" "It's me."
Memories, versions, voices come to an end,
the stairs, rooms, buildings all gone too,
you on the third floor buzzing me in.

ONE SUNDAY NIGHT

One Sunday night at home all alone
in the century just before this one
I read in the *Tribune's* science section
that the universe is endless, here forever,
but the earth will be destroyed, whether
by burning or freezing I don't remember,
and I felt so alone I had to call you,
and you were home alone too, and you
assured me of your love, and I, you
of mine, but in less than a year
we broke up, and in the next year
each married someone else and we never
met again, though I heard you moved far
away, but I never knew exactly where.

YOU TURNED

We finally stopped talking, you tired
of all that, and, agreeing to the terms
the god laid down, we climbed back up
toward earth, to where we had been before,
where I had lost you... now no more talking or
looking at each other until we got there.
But I wanted to talk further, and turned
toward you—to ask, to have you clarify,
to find out still more, to understand
at last, to know, to see, to grasp...
But I saw your tired look as you turned,
and I stared at the curved back of your hand—
a faint wave, or your hand startled upward
by that abrupt turn your body made, or your
hand almost trying to shield your ear.

SPOUSE

Two aides from Uganda and one from Tanzania
know you more intimately than I do these days.
They change you, wash you, wipe you, serve you.
I should, but won't, or can't, or mustn't.
I've turned you over to the Senior Helpers,
green carders from Africa settled in Waltham.
While they cook or mop up I work on my lines
or take my walks or have lunch with friends.
When they undress you for bed or for a shower
I take a peek at your body, wizened and weak.
What's happening to you has versions in myself.
You know what's going on, but I don't know
if you are angry or resigned or just plain sad.
It's all "get me now," or ask, hear the answer,
ask again. I repeat, go louder, vary my words.
I've even taken to writing the answers down.

CUSTER'S LAST STAND

Bound in by the bed rail, he rumped,
hipped, thighed, elbowed, heeled, fingered
his way down to the foot of the bed where
his dangling toes twitched for the floor
where he teetered and lurched and stretched
toward the wheelchair's handlebars, his shaking
hands reaching and clutching those bent horns,
finished and ribbed for the gripping, and
he pushed the chair as if it were a walker.
"Stay in bed, the aide'll come in the morning,
you're double-padded for the night," a wife
wailed from her side of the Queen Size,
but he barked over his right shoulder,
"Nobody has a right to bar me in bed
and keep me from going to pee. I'm not
asking for help, I can go by myself."
He pushed the black chair, bumping the hamper,
steering 'round the bend and down the hallway,
re-inventing the wheelchair. It was as if
he was pushing himself, the invisible sitter,
as he gained on the night-light toward
the other one in the room he was headed for.

ROWEN-LOVE

The shames, the failings owned-up-to now
invite the two of us to give ourselves
to each other again, though not exactly
the way we did when we were back in college.
We still have the hots but not the liquids.
In facing what went wrong we get to see
how our failures hatched one another.
Our bodies sag and falter, yet our
candor now is our late grasp of what
we read in Yeats in our junior year,
"the tragedy of sexual intercourse
is the perpetual virginity of the soul."
We're old and glad to be in touch again, though
I detect your ever so slight distancing—
protecting yourself, prepping for loss.

OUT AT THE CAPE

Sitting on the steps leading down to the lawn
where the plastic clothespins spring-clipped
nothing except themselves to the vacant line,
I suddenly saw those wooden clothespins—
smooth-grained, fork-leggèd and derby-headed—
that my mother used to wedge into the clothesline,
a braided rope also good for making knots or
playing jump rope or grabbing in tug of war, the line
she strung out near the pulley mounted above the gray
clothespin bag, wide and deep as a sower's sack.
Then those wooden, cleft figurettes disappeared
and I returned to staring, beyond the volley ball net,
at the foliage that marked the end of our property—
leaves and brake and bush and stems and viny things
so dense I couldn't see through it all, nothing but
that wilding wall of green with gaps of darkness.
I was looking for the answer to my question, "What
should I do now? Was I through now? Was I out of poems?
Have I lost my powers, time now to lie down and die?"
And all I did was sit, staring at the silent green.

III

FROM *GREEN AQUARIUM*

1

THE DEATH OF AN OX

"You raise my horn high like that of a wild ox...." Psalm 92:11

With burning horns—two twisted candles under a beaming yellow halo—with a hoarse bellow, an ox plunges out of a burning stable, as if a gold ritual slaughtering knife was stuck in his throat. The drying dung glued to his rear end smokes in violet clumps on the ground, dung smeared above his hoofs, his flesh the flames of burning wild grass.

The first falling snow—as if someone chased a large flock of pearl-white young doves from a turbulent sky, driving them down to the sinful earth and into a hot sleep— the snow is unable to extinguish the fire. When the sparks—flying red needles—pierce the falling doves there is no sustained cry—"oy"—and the doves are swallowed by the eager fire. And in the midst of its onslaught on the devoured snow- doves, the fire rages even wilder. Joyfully the fire, forged in the ox's copper ribs, sits like a frenzied naked satyr on the back of the ox, lashing him with pyre-whips.

A "mmmoo" carries to the ox's ears—a shuddering, a longing, a thunder of chopped-off wings.

He cannot reply. His mouth is open. The tongue gone.

His momentum drives him further —fire lifts from the earth, from the sunset- dark swamp that stretches into a large lake.

Then when he storms into the lake up to his knees, his double elliptical eyes— like glass of many colors fused together—catch sight of another ox in the water, one opposite him, with downward burning horns in a sky under him, the wrinkles in its face becoming a smile on a human face.

His copper ribs burst apart.

The snow falls and falls.

And the ox twists his head to the left, in the direction of his home village, where only a dark chimney remains, like a dead hand that cannot gesture or touch.

Meanwhile, the horns continue to burn, like candles at the head of a corpse, and die out with the day.

2

IN MEMORY OF A FUR JACKET

In becoming a fur jacket you remained a lamb.

When my mother bartered a bag of salt for you with a hundred year old Kyrgyz man and delighted me with the present for my seventh birthday—it was as if my mother's breath had entered my bones, as if I had put on a living sun...

Cross-eyed and gashed by daggers the days marched through the snows. In you I created my first poem—a snowman.

I was a spirit in your wings. Disappeared from myself. Seven radiant doves brought me home.

You accompanied me over times, lands, with melodies from my childhood — a warm violin.

You saw how the north star had scratched me...

When I outgrew you, your hands—the two sleeves—gave themselves to me to prolong the friendship.

To you, my fur jacket, I confided my moonstruck pieces of paper, with their blind jumpy lines, like the staggering of a drunkard in snow...

And later, when my dovecote was gone with the clouds, who else but you and a pack of wounds accompanied me!...

When my face alternated with a clenched finger you didn't allow the pale blue ice to congeal my smile.

And once at night in a forest, over snakes embalmed in ice, a woman went into labor, and in you, in your warm nest, a blue child appeared—as blue as you.

And a second time, naked, except for you on my shoulders, I rode to the morning sun over a battlefield.

The snow—a pure nocturnal sky. My horse—an anthem over snow. Golden fishes pour out of the slash in its veiny neck. My ribs are covered with its ribs. Skin is superfluous. You also became superfluous. Did you sense my struggle and, like a glance blue with wisdom, lower yourself into the snow?

A horse reared. Its rider caught sight of a blue lamb—wandering in eternity: "Meh—meh... mah—meh..."

And a wolf in the snow—a gleaming, sharpened knife with four feet—harvests the fields.

THE LAST ONE

—Moyshe-Leyb Halpern

Evening sun.
And all the flies in the corners of the windows,
in the evening cold—
congealed—
maybe already dead—
and on the edge of the water glass—the last one,
alone in the whole room—and
I say, "Sing me something about your distant homeland,
dear fly."
I hear her weeping as she answers me:
may her right foot wither
if she strikes up a tune
by these foreign waters
and if she forgets
that dear dunghill
that once was her homeland—

RICHARD III AGAIN

After Richmond kills Richard, and Richmond,
wearing the crown that sat on Richard's head,
does his "our-national-nightmare-is-over" speech,
all the characters in the play come back on stage,
however small or great their roles had been,
as walls half-descend toward the stage, each
wall draped with white towels hanging from a rack,
and all the actors stretch upward toward the towels,
the clean white towels shining out of reach.

2018

AT THE STAKE

She took out her knife
and cut the guylines
knotted to their stakes.
The tent collapsed,
smothering acrobats,
clowns, lions, and hawkers
hawking their treats
up and down the aisles.
Richard Learnéd told her
what all the Master Works show—
"Enchanted to a stone"—
but she replied, "Can't read
right now; will, when done,
when we've won our rights,"
and drove in the new stakes,
and pulled on the new ropes,
and called for the new acts.

2018

PHILOSOPHER'S STONE

("Hilary Putnam was one of the greatest philosophers
this country has ever produced."
Martha C. Nussbaum)

I can't read you, Hilary, though your table talk must have equaled
Coleridge's or Dr. Johnson's. Your vigorous quips—
"The function of sex is to have grandchildren"; "God doesn't know God"—
turned personal, re-shaped in the garbs of my own obsessions:
My deterioration in old age stares at the bodies that are growing;
If God is a puzzle to Himself how can I (or anyone) speak in His name?
You left traces in my mind like seeds on receptive ground.
Like a young Abraham you threw yourself into your beliefs, at the end
bolstered up in a hospital bed angled into a study,
touched by and touching back children and grandchildren around you,
bestowing last-breath blessings gentler than those of the Patriarchs,
smiling at and saying "hello" to the three Haitian women
in their agency-blue, trained both to be nearby and to hover in the background.

Yet I can't read you, Hilary—"Philosophy must be scientific,"
your former student said you said. For us ordinaries—
we poets, social workers, rabbis, physicians, lawyers, architects—
you might as well have been a scientist, for around
the shabbes candles (you lit), the challah (you baked), the wine (you
          selected), the fish (you prepared), the dessert (you concocted)
you so explained String Theory that I thought I understood it;
then you read to us, showing why Louis MacNeice was one of your favorite poets,
but when you dismissed Santayana or played down Nietzsche—I thought—
just the philosopher poets like to read. Then you sailed off again,
quoting *Middlemarch*, musing on Paris in the 20s, praising the Southern
          Poverty Law Center.

Yet I can't read you, Hilary, as I can James or Dewey,
you the only polymath I have ever known, and when you encompassed
Jews and Judaism the walls of parochialism crashed down to reveal the
        waiting city.
Even when, I red-facedly admit, I was afraid to argue with you,
I breathed in your words—learning, learning, enjoying, sent back to
        experience and reading; yet

I can't read you, Hilary—though I tried out your choices in wines,
cheeses, coffees, movies, recipes, admired your ability to sail,
and listened hard when you breathed life into dull passages of Talmud, you
polymath with the common touch, soul-mind with whom we reasoned and sang.

Yet I can't read you, Hilary. For me your best "thought experiments"
        were around the challah Friday nights.
It didn't matter then that I can't read you, Hilary.
Oh, major man, you who knew the chemistries of gusto,
your life possessed an art I want to know even more than to read you.

April, 2016

FALL MORNING

A drip-leaf spectacle takes me by surprise when
I open my door to the porch to get my copy of the *Times*
and then I go down to take a closer look at the leaves
and enjoy their having fallen into a dispersed stickiness
as if I had been waiting for them to relieve me of the daily news
or a call to the pharmacy or the arrivals of my wife's aides.
For a moment the raindrop luster of each car's body stuns me,
 the metals blistered into light, a speckled auto show alongside
        the curb.
Then I find myself wondering how I make a poem of this,
my pleasure like each seam halving its leaf
and then turning into a nib just past the leaf itself.

BORROWED TIME

The happiest time of my day
is when I wake and can't tell
which sleep it was, though
what I'm wearing can
or the light or the dark
seeping through the blinds
or the black hands tapering
toward numbers on the white face;
then I'm grateful yet sorry—
in the know and no longer
in that time I couldn't tell.

DOORKNOB

("A man's road back to himself is a return from his spiritual exile,
for that is what a personal history amounts to—exile."

Saul Bellow, *The Actual*)

Back to whom? Return from whom?

It must be a return to the person you never were
but the person you knew you could have been,
the one you failed to be, or feared to be, and in
The Actual Harry returns also to a woman who
once might have helped him, but, back then, was in
her own exile, the two, back then, in their tense love.

It must be Kafka at the door he never went through,
when he lacked the key or the courage to turn the knob
or the urge to push the door, and it never opened
freely, swinging out on the hinges, giving access,
entry to hallway, rooms. Yet there was a knob
even Kafka finally learned to turn with Dora's help.

It must be Wilhelm in *Seize the Day* who,
when he looks at the corpse in the chapel,
cries his eyes out for a dead stranger,
the lost life of a man laid out, a man
he never knew, a man who cannot rise
from his coffin, while Wilhelm, broke, jobless,
foolish, is alone, lost, staring at the body
lying there, among the mourners in the funeral home.
Back to whom? Return from whom?
It must be me thinking of all the times, Evelyn,
I passed the funeral home further down your block
on my way to the subway after leaving
your apartment between Columbus and Amsterdam.

46

NO NEVER

I will never let Joyce Baum get any money.
My father never saw her in those three years
he was dying, all that time I lived with him,
cared for him, as he needed me more and more.
I had to make sure he didn't slip in the shower.
I locked her out. *I* answered the telephone.
She couldn't even claim her clothes.
I will never let Joyce Baum get any money.
He always meant to change that old will.
In the end he counted on me to take him
where he had to go, and I always brought
him back to the living room, the bedroom.
In his love for me, in his need for me,
I deserve that money, not Joyce Baum,
and I tell you this so you will win
my case, and I get the money I deserve.
I know you're going to say, "But Beverly,
I can only present what a court is willing
to hear, what is relevant to the case."
I will never let Joyce Baum get any money
even though (once) he loved her for herself,
while he loved me for what I did for him.
In all of Berkeley my father possessed
the greatest collection of English fiction.
And I read through it all, and it pleased him
I could talk to him about it. Joyce Baum
didn't do that with him. Nor did she have
the kind of education I had at Reed.
But you know, I don't want the award
for the greatest affectionate daughter.
I just wanted his love for myself alone.
No one knows what I went through, how I

helped him as he became helpless, wasted away.
I read to him from his shelves of novels.
I knew which one he wanted, I fingered it out,
read it for as long as he was willing, then
jiggled it back into place, where it belonged.
No one knows how many ways I had to help him.
Not even you with, "I can imagine."

A VELVET DRESS

—Moyshe-Leyb Halpern

The young lady in bed stood on her head
and with her naked feet in the air
burst into tears, like a squall—
"A velvet dress, a velvet dress!"
The old woman with closed sleepy eyes
promised to buy her a great brass trumpet
so she could puff up her cheeks
and blow into it whenever she wants.
But that didn't satisfy
the young lady in bed who stood on her head.
Her naked feet twisted in the air like a bagel,
she kept on insisting—
"A velvet dress, a velvet dress!"
The old woman opened her eyes and softly
promised her, "If you would only go to sleep
I will buy you the red flute from the shepherd
which makes sounds like doo-doo and doodle-a-doo."
It looked like the young lady in bed who stood on her head
had almost forgotten the velvet dress—
her naked feet, her hands stretched out in wild childish joy,
waving them in front, waving them at the side—
until she reminded herself once more.
And with her crazy feet flailing in the air
the young lady in bed who stood on her head
kept insisting, "A velvet dress,
a velvet dress!" And nothing but.

FROM A LOST POEM

Unshorn, abstinent, austere lifter of weights,
Samson, even before his birth, was allotted his life by a nameless angel.
Heroes do have a way of being marked from the cradle or even earlier,
like Jacob and Moses and Joseph and Abraham, just to stick to one tribe,
all steered toward later tasks, their having a nationalized childhood.
But God and His messenger-angel have chosen a manchild of the wrong
        temperament—
Samson can't bear his divine assignment, can't resist displays.
God and His angel have rushed too quickly to delegate a fate.
Then rashness and scorn and even Samson's own civil war seem necessary—
compelling and half beautiful in ways we half understand.

IV

THE MOUTH OF UNCLE MAX

I

The brassy glare of a gold tooth socketed in his lower gum
branded the Yiddish my Uncle Max expelled—
his nugget-tooth exhibiting an alien luster,
his hands gesticulating his sounds in the living room,
his clack grating that sheeny element into my food,
and when he gloated or argued I could see the ridges of his enamels
and amalgams cratered all the way to the back of his mouth.
His sounds conspired with the tribal radio station
my father dialed up on Sunday mornings, with
the chatterboxes in the stores, with the pitch of the
fruit and vegetable peddler guiding his nag
by the throatlatch down the streets of our neighborhood,
with the supplicant *shray* of the old man in the alley—
"Kesh-Kloze, Kesh-Kloze"—offering money for old clothes
and rags, his Yiddish-English clamoring into my ears.
My mother calls down, asking him up to our apartment.
What are these sounds? What are they doing to me?
Why must I protect myself from this old world
seeping into me, from these sounds snaring me,
from that alloyed tooth implanted in Uncle Max's mouth?

II

I can't understand why Yiddish has such a hold on me—
Ikh ken nit farshteyn far vos yidish hot aza onkhap af mir.
Yiddish, what did I run away from when I ran away from you?

What did I embrace when finally, in my forties, I embraced you?
You are more than speech; you are what went into the making of me.
I can see again Uncle Max's tooth—how gross and garish it was,
how repulsive and conjuring, how primitive and configured—
that brazen gold that threatened me, that seized me,
that glary yellow grinder that flashed way back in his mouth,
where accents hive, gauche habits thrive, and the old world lurks—
that source and cruncher of sounds, that grasp, that *onkhap*.

YIDDISH MOVES

I felt the tug of Yiddish and the taste of it, kitchen-depth of kin-speech,
sensed it in the shelf paper, linoleum, oilcloth, doilies, curtains, shades,
traced it in the lippy edges of the couch's cushions, in the seam of the bolster,
watched it in the flies flecking the sticky paper coiling down from the ceiling;
carried it in my childhood body in the cramped apartment, my own body
penetrated by *mame loshn*, and Yiddish turned into remnant
nerve endings and vesicles, became my unskilled native tongue
lurking in me in the midst of my high school-college readings of Whitman,
       James, Dreiser, Eliot,
my seedtime analyses and affinities driven by my very condition of disparity
and otherness, my outsider moods and minds tempered by the aboriginal
and canny twists and turns of the Yiddish joke, its digging under assumptions,
its honed mockery of patrician maneuvers, of goyish satisfactions,
of civic swindlings, of boastings, calibrations of power, smugness of gain—
oh, gift of gab tempered into skepticism, pitched into us-vs.-them, moaned
       into pathos of loss,
oh, language of pity, of voluptuous sarcasm, of love and rebuke of God,
(giving back to Him what He hurled at the people in Hebrew),
oh, language of diminishment either taunting or tender, oh lilt of endearment,
       bravura of the blessing-curse,
oh, tongue inclined to the calling of account, tribal language of reckoning,
       dismissed tongue that assessed the world,
oh, mawkish tongue, purveyor of schmaltz that blocks the arteries of candor,
you, bathos-speech deserving the ridicule and scorn of your own mocking powers,
oh, vernacular of moving hands, of gargled modulations, garrulity nosying
       into its own ruminations,
oh, challah-speech pinched off and chewed over in the kitchen, around the table
and inside the child's mouth, intellect and taste—eating-speech—
oh, language of early years, the child's ears subject to the elementary sound-school,
zhargon elbowing, spurring, coloring, nudging, noodging, devising, claiming,

oh, Yiddish, a language without a land and you paid for it, a language born
        to pity and to probe,
your genius of the declarative sentence attuned to the interrogative—"You
        call this coffee"—
Yiddish feeding into English as rhythm, vocabulary, tone, syntax,
while I became the heir and spender of memory, the inheritor-delver
into the drawers, the valises, the trunks, the shoulder bags, finding
        there dear coinage,
even as you, Yiddish, were slipping away, only to flavor America.

DOWN WITH YIDDISH

Its sounds enliven its own demise,
words in the breath of their very loss,
like leaves shaken by gusts of wind
until the stems on the branches break
loose and all the leaves all fall down, we
attuned to the very process of that going.
Meanwhile, the up-to-date terminologies
by Yiddish lexicographers for those engaged
in stockmarket, stadium, laboratory
are mere contrivances, ingenious and unspoken.
Glatshteyn, Sutzkever, Moyshe-Leyb—
show me the depths of Yiddish I love
to hear myself sounding in my throat,
your genius of speech still vibrating
and spiraling from my ear to my brain.
Glatshteyn, Sutzkever, Moyshe-Leyb—
show me your letters, words, rhythms
still able to transport me to the world,
my body resounding to your tones,
the way lovers are touched by the sounds
they make, touched here, touched there,
or the way anyone exposed to history
learns how loss feeds upon loss. Or doesn't.

I remember that afternoon at the 92nd Street Y
when you and I started chatting after seeing
a restored Yiddish film with new subtitles,
with lost scenes respliced for this version,
and we went to your apartment on the West Side,

where you read to me your Yiddish poems
and you showed me what, decades earlier,
you had rescued from Cracow and packed deeper
than Customs looked when you came through,
you now giving me a tutorial (*a privateh lektsieh*)
in the flesh, lip-to-lip corrections, tongue flexed,
the language inventive, exhaustive in our usage.

SPORADIC VISITANT...

(after Avrom Sutzkever's last poem in *Twin Brother*)

Sporadic visitant,
release sounds, impressions
confined within me,
tongs or tweezers
plucking them out of me

Sporadic visitant,
outsource my sources,
assume whatever forms agree with you,
reach in as far back as you need,
as long as you transfer what you grip,
I then stronger from the strongest pain,
stronger from the first love,
stronger from the last love,
as you pry, clutch and issue

Sporadic visitant,
perhaps you are the Tree of Life
extending its limbs towards me
outside the window
so I can reach out and touch a twig,
the tree giving forth from its innerness,
trusting its textures from trunk to tip,
containing epitomes of forest,
my own mind foraging in the brush of itself

Sporadic visitant,
Sutzkever's figments of Yiddish,
Genesis-Tree of speech—

vines sinuating on branches,
sky punctuating leaves,
lichens modifying wood

Sporadic visitant—
translate me
translating Sutzkever

PRIMAL YIDDISH

You shift from strokes and stipples into letters and syllables
as my eyes and tongue follow you word by word, line by line.
Your hooks, curves, flecks, loops, dents, squares
transfigure into tones, drifts, hints, inklings—
your glyphic talents lurking in you even as my fingertips
are barely touching the paper under your forms and spacings,
my fingertips inching from the right side of the page
toward the gutter margin or away from that runnel
toward the left edge of the page as your designs
make their way down the pages into words, phrasings,
lines, stanzas—a poem, a second poem, a third.
How generant for me that no matter how much I read you
I cannot simply slide across your surface and fluently
figure out your intentions, suggestions, sonants,
but slowly sense a sort of fremitus as my fingertips
brush along the bottom of your letterings and flections.
This permanent striving to know you within the gestures
of your shapes—letters notched, bent, repossessed
through thick and thin—is like being in love with somebody
revealing herself through her moving contours, unlike English,
which has clearly abstracted itself into sound and meaning.
Yiddish letters—I taste you as you substantiate your shapes
        and meanings.
And then sometimes all that close study of you pays off
instantly and you leap off the sheet right into
my eyes and ears and mouth—a physiology of knowing—
as when reading Anna Margolin's crafting of an edgy
conversation between a man and a woman, how the unspoken
and the spoken intimate each other—in her poem "Entracte."

Like my own life I have known you and not known you
ever since I can first remember seeing you or hearing you,
puzzled at the way you infiltrated my body, insisting
you were of my world, you both inside of me and
speech and sounds brought to me, you my native tongue
strange to me, you innate, seeping in, emanating—
tribal sounds sizzling in the vessels on the gas range.
Yiddish letters—I give up. There is nothing else
for me to write about. The permanent striving to know you
within the exactions of your shapes is what a woman's body
has always seemed to me—provoker, bearer, other.
Despite all that you have gone through you are made for me,
you what I must seek, I both taken and puzzled by you
and then taken by you where all of your intimations lead me.
It was I who had to come back to you and did and did, even
though some pulse of you may still hide from me, escape me.
I need to come into my known and unknown by touching you,
by sounding you out, absorbing your body, fleck by fleck, *fleknvayz*...

ENTRACTE

—Anna Margolin

The delicate weave of clever conversation,
like cobwebs quivering from a breeze,
suddenly tore apart.
Marvelling, leisurely smiling,
she sensed him
through the charged rustling silence
the way one might sense a wolf while sleeping:
its golden bloodshot eyes,
taut ribs,
firm, bent paws,
the wolf dizzyingly closing in around her,
circling and circling nearer.
Marvelling, leisurely smiling,
with disgust and with a sweet shudder
she tasted wolf-blood
between her teeth.
And she slowly bent her head— showing him the hot, wearied
whites of her eyes—
slowly bent,
while assembling
the incisive words of the cool conversation.

DER FRUKHTBOYM

The tree that once grew various fruits
cannot grow any new fruits anymore
but only hold the fruits it grew before.
Anyone can come, and from anywhere,
to pluck a fruit and eat it right there.
Even after they are plucked, the fruits
still remain where they hung before.
No one knows if the tree is alive or dead
or if the tree is both alive and dead.

V

A PROFESSOR RE-READING *CALAMUS* (1967)

How could I have taken so long to understand you, Walt?
How could I not have known what you were about?
How could I not have seen why poetry was not enough for you?
How could I have read you and read you and not have possessed you?
I failed to take you literally, failed to take you at your true word,
failed by taking you for democratic oracle, national prophet, hymnist
        of brotherhood,
I abstracting "camerado," "companion," "brother," "lover,"
abstracting "the new person drawn to me," "the one I love," "comrade lover,"
abstracting "Calamus taste," "tongue aromatic," "herbage of my breast."
Forgive my conversions of you to professings of democracy, to escapist-ideals,
forgive my tenured life that failed to see all you were angling towards,
        readying for, desired.
Oh, how removed I was from all that was amorous and fluid and pressing
        in your lines,
oh, how off-base my notions about you—the evasions in my teaching, my book,
        my life—
oh, Walt, I, the teacher of reading, myself never knew how to read,
only now seeing that you even turned the dead Lincoln into the lost camerado.
Oh, now on the edge of retirement I become free to read you truly and even see
how *you* in all your editions and shifting of poems and re-writings
        and omissions,
how *you* in all your selves' effusions and obscure hintings of an unrevealed life,
how *you* in your kaballah-like code for the initials of a lover,
how *you* in all your mutations and entertainings of multitudes
were giving off signs you were afraid of your self, of being exposed, of being
        spotted behind the blinds.
So, you misled me, as I misled myself, as you misled yourself,
so, it turns out we are closer than either of us imagined,
so, you look under my boot soles with me and we see our lives revealed,

so, Walt, you and I are now turned into camerados, new persons drawn to
    one another,
we two old men ready to accompany each other, to walk the shoreline, where
    the last bubbles of spume reach our insteps.

HERE'S LOOKING AT YOU, WHITMAN

That portrait of you, the one in the 1855 edition, from an engraving
       after a daguerreotype—
you don't look like a teamster, or a Missourian crossing the plains,
you don't look like "one of the roughs... disorderly, fleshy and sensual,"
you don't look like someone who's had sex with the earth or the ocean or
       the wind or his own soul.
Your right arm loosely akimbo and your left doing nothing but poking
       into a pocket,
you hardly look like someone with "polish'd and perfect limbs."
That triangle of red flannel just below the neck, pointed to by the trimmed beard,
summons up "I lie in the night in my red shirt," you yourself one of
       "The Sleepers."
The rumply debonair air, the slight, inviting slouch—*Walt Whitman depicting
       himself in his carpenter's garb*—you,
the intrigant, the stagey loafer—a few steps down from the *flaneur* or
       up from the drugged lounger—you,
in that "impalpable certain rest," pending, tarrying, you, in your sly posture,
sexless or multi-sexual, I can't tell which, you, coming on or waiting
       for the come-on,
you not at all like, or secretly like, the one who warns, "my firelock
       leaned in the corner,"
you not at all like, or secretly like, "the comrade of raftsmen and coalmen"
       you say you are,
you the ego-slinger for hire, who will travel anywhere, in and out of anyone,
you are the greatest practitioner of metamorphosis since Ovid—Demos-Proteus.

I actually looked for you under my Brooks Addiction Walking Shoe,
scraping the sole with a paring knife, poking, angling, among the ridges
       and smutch.
Oh, you dissembler, there and not there, yet I had an inkling of your approval

of the lavish act of scraping the sole.
Where are you, Walt, you who disappear in the body of your poem,
        waiting for me to get inside of it?
Where are you, Walt, in that portrait of you, from an engraving after
        a daguerreotype,
you who stand atilt on the frontispiece, so openly furtive and patient?

WHITMAN/VITMAN

If you had been Velvl Vitman, I'd have
turned your Yiddish into English, I
poking around in the circuits of your beard,
my fingers finding and tracing your face,
my palms grazing your ruddy flesh,
your body and movements affecting me
and my characters, my strokes, and my lines;
the tones of the syllables, and pauses,
and the corresponding flecks of our words
make a marriage between us, my English
coming off of your Yiddish, tongue to tongue,
you then closer to me than ever before.
Of if I was Ruvn-Yankev Fayn and you still
Walt Whitman, I'd have turned your English
into Yiddish, showing how the body
of a poem could turn into another body,
the two of us closer than ever,
the way V inheres in W.

IN DELMORE AGAIN

Tonight, while reading your poems, Delmore,
I notice two straw colored hairs
sticking out from the base of my left thumb,
on its side as it presses the page,
those hairs just grazing two of the lines
from your poem about curing souls, "Far Rockaway":
"That nervous conscience amid the concessions
Is a haunting, haunted moon."
Delmore, my hairs on your poem make me think
of how you and I and Whitman come from Brooklyn.
How long I have wanted to know you both,
and in some sense I imagine I do.
Your being well or not means a lot to me,
Delmore. To my thoughts about poetry, what it takes.
Now, putting down your book,
taking the last pills before going to bed,
I look out of our dark kitchen
at the house next door, black windows
receding into themselves, all dark there,
except where the moon strikes the flashing,
a lunar chute glaring to the gutter.

READING BOOK XI
OF *PARADISE LOST*

On an evening that means a lot to others,
Christmas Eve, I am moved to tears
by Angel Michael's herbal cures
of Adam's eyes, removing a cataract
induced by Satan, opening Adam's eyes
to the world he is about to enter
since he's been expelled from Paradise,
Milton inventing this visionary moment
though his own eyes have gone dark, beyond
all help, while Adam is invited to open his.

How come I hadn't seen the pity of this moment
the times I'd read the poem before, seen Milton's
presence in his generant gift to Adam?
And now this evening means something further,
something other than an evening-that-means-
a-lot-to-others, one dearer to me now
because I see Milton anew, hear him anew,
the scene stemming from rue and eyebright,
myself entranced by the plants Milton
employs, found in formulary and psalm.

NORTHEAST CORRIDOR

Once, riding Amtrak from Boston to Penn Station to read my translations
      in New York,
I saw the ghosts of Yiddish poets wearing furrowed mantles and coming
      out from behind trees
somewhere north of New Haven and asking me to translate them,
and I wrote a poem about their emergence and their approaching the train
      and letting me know they gave me sanction.
Now I imagine they come from the woods again and invite me to join them,
      to go back among the trees with them.
"Read your poems to us," their leader urged, "and because you have
      translated our poems into English
we will return the favor and translate your poems into Yiddish and you
      will become part of our *brudershaft.*
And thus that very language you once wanted least to do with
now becomes that language you need most of all. Come, talk with us."
Their leader, whom I knew had an elegant English, because we chatted once
      in a restaurant on East 86th St., near YIVO,
extended his invitation in Yiddish, trusting I would understand, as I
      once did over our coffee.
And the gravelly, clamant-alien voices of the old men of my childhood
      changed into the leader's kind offer.
"Come," he invited me again, "come with us back into the woods where
      you can talk with us"—
Kum, kum mit undz tsurik in vald vu du kenst redn mit undz—
and as I followed the others moving deeper into the woods their mantles
      changed into the barks of trees.

LOVE LINES IN OLD AGE

(for Bert Stern)

If you were a woman I would steal you from your husband,
or if we were gay I would have an affair with you,
but we're two old Jews, straight, in a manner of speaking,
who dutifully got their Ph.D.s, taught, had kids,
and kept their passion for poetry—reading it, writing it.
I love Whitman a bit more than you do.
You love Blake a bit more than I do,
but we both stick by Yeats; and Wordsworth and Hardy.
You're drawn to the Buddha; I'm still entwined in the Jewish Bible.
You smile at the way the grass bends when an army invades and the way
        it bends when that army retreats, as you read in Du Fu,
while I am stuck on the hot coal the angel's hand lays on Isaiah's lips.
We hold our love in our differences and in our contradictions.

To think, I have lived long enough to fall in love with a guy in old age.
So, *this* is Calamus, without "the love-flesh swelling."
You keep me going. I keep you going. Poetry keeps us going.
We gas each other up, pump up each other, feed off of each other.
It's like Whitman rocking in his chair on Mickle St. in Camden,
and his long looked-for camerado finally shows up and they go at
        their gabbing, just as we do:
the achievement of Pound—that son of a bitch; the Red Sox;
the beauty of Tennyson when he's lost his faith; fascism in America;
David Ferry's gorgeous translations; the women's movement; what is free verse?
How differently we write—you patiently waiting for nature to reveal itself,
I wrestling with a night spirit until I am bent into a new name.
And then sometimes you write a bit like me and I a bit like you.
How we both adore the necks of Degas' women, and how we still ache
        over the fall of Delmore Schwartz.

And we tell each other our dreams, like exchanging poems—
mine of a carboy seated in the corner of an empty room, crated so
        as to safeguard its corrosives,
yours of sitting on a porch in your beloved Adirondacks,
watching squirrels' tails divest and a plumed scamper turn into a
        naked scuttle.

Despite lagging energies, the blanks, the slippages,
how long I have waited for you.
I feel like a kid skipping home from kindergarten
and breathlessly telling his mother,
"I, I made a new friend today.
We're gonna' be friends for life.
He, he invited me over.
I, I invited him over.
His name is Bert."

NOTES

"Quotation Poem"—The passage by Proust is translated by André Aciman.

"A Word in the Mouth"—Levi-Yitzkhok of Berdichev (1740-1809), a Hasidic Leader, was known for the succor he gave poor Jews and his advocacy for them before God.

"Northeast Corridor"—YIVO is a research institute in New York devoted to the study of Yiddish and East European Jewish life.

ACKNOWLEDGEMENTS

Acknowledgement is made to the editors of the journals where the following poems originally appeared:

Asymptote: "Prayer," "A Word in the Mouth," "The Last One," "Kol Kidre," "The Velvet Dress," "In Central Park."

Battery Journal: "The Death of an Ox," "Down with Yiddish," "The Mouth of Uncle Max," "Reading Book XI of *Paradise Lost*."

Free Inquiry: "One Sunday Night."

Ibbetson Street: "From a Lost Poem."

In geveb: "Yiddish Moves."

Jewish Currents: "Entracte."

Mudfish: "To a Woman Remembered," "Northeast Corridor," "Love Lines in Old Age," and "Out at the Cape."

The Poetry Porch: "American Heritage Dictionary of the English Language," "Philosopher's Stone," "Farewell," "Jacobo and Paulina," and "Stickball."

"Soradic visitant..." appeared as an appendix to my translations *The Full Pomegranate: Poems of Avrom Sutzkever* (SUNY Press).

"A Professor Re-Reading *Calamus* (1967)," "Here's Looking at You, Whitman," and "Whitman/Vitman" appeared in my chapbook *Whitman/Vitman* (Finishing Line Press).

Once again, I am pleased to thank George Kalogeris, Marcia Karp, and Bert Stern for their help in my shaping the book.

I am grateful again to Ruth Wisse for giving me permission to include my new translations of poems by Avrom Sutzkever.

I thank Solon Beinfeld once more for his help with my translations of Yiddish poetry.

Photo by Miriam Fein-Cole

Richard J. Fein has published eleven books of poetry. His book *Kafka's Ear* has won the Maurice English Award. He has also published three books of his translations of Yiddish poetry: Selected Poems of *Yankev Glatshteyn; With Everything We've Got; The Full Pomegranate: Poems of Avrom Sutzkever.* And he has also published three books of prose: *Robert Lowell,* a critical study; The Dance of *Leah,* a memoir of Yiddish; *Yiddish Genesis*, personal essays.

He was born in Brooklyn, New York. He taught at Hunter College and the University of Puerto Rico before teaching many years at SUNY, New Paltz. He also spent a year on a Fulbright in India, teaching American literature.

Praise for *Losing It*

The modern Yiddish poets ("Glatshteyn, Sutzkever, Moyshe-Leyb— / show me your letters, words, rhythms") are the spiritual guides to Richard Fein's fine new book, which has a kind of Jewish saudade—a bittersweet nostalgia not just for something gone, but also a yearning for what might have been. *Losing It* is a book that beautifully pinpoints its lost worlds.

> **Edward Hirsch, author of *Gabriel* and**
> ***Stranger by Night***

In his childhood poem *"The Mouth of Uncle Max"* the poet recalls:

> The brassy glare of a gold tooth socketed in his lower gum
> branded the Yiddish my Uncle Max expelled–
> his nugget tooth exhibiting an alien luster...

English and Yiddish are the pincer jaws of this magnificent book that holds us in the grip of its linguistic conviction even as it expresses a lyric disenchantment. Richard Fein's poetry is the gold standard of how a poet-translator can be both deeply at home, and so tellingly estranged, in two forms of speech, as when the Yiddish words "expelled" from an uncle's mouth take on a sublimely uncanny "alien luster" in English. *Losing It* is the work of an American master.

> **George Kalogeris, author of *Guide to Greece***

"The heir and spender of memory," a treasurer of sense and experience, of the innocence of touch and smell and taste, Richard Fein offers us the wealth of feelings and perceptions ever refined by his love of life and his mastery of language. A clairvoyant of the ordinary, Fein sees into the life of objects and people, his living hand, warm and capable, dissemi-nates acute details that right before our eyes grow into real presences: "the way lovers are touched by the sounds\ they make."

> **Shahar Bram, author of *Portraits & Photographs***

Praise for *Losing It*

I love the book. Just look at the very simple poem called "Out at the Cape," where Richard Fein sits on the back steps looking at clothespins and then in a phrase appropriate to a visionary experience, "I suddenly saw," and what he sees is the vision where he carefully describes the clothespins mysteriously attached only to themselves. Then he has the memory of his mother pulling the braided rope of a clothesline and then of rope jumping and rope for tug of war. Then, in a language appropriate to visionary experience, "those wooden, cleft figurettes disappeared." Not a whole lot to it, maybe, but what there is is beautifully realized, and the poet, if not at first the reader, is ready for the big surprise. He sees the volleyball net and beyond it the foliage that marked the end of the property, "that wilding wall of green with gaps of darkness." And suddenly he tells us (me the reader and he the writer), the visionary experience having disappeared:

> I was looking for the answer to my question, "What
> should I do now? Was I through now? Was I out of poems?
> Have I lost my powers, time now to lie down and die?"
> And all I did was sit, staring at the silent green.

It's the right there now of these poems, as if he's talking to me the reader and to himself at the very moment when the poem was happening. This is true of everybody's writing of poems but very vividly and immediately of this poem and the poems in this beautiful book. He's right there at the moment when he wrote the lines about the clothespins on the lines vacant of laundry, a vision of clotheslineness. The vision disappears and then he has that extraordinary response to the vision and its disappearance.

Thank God he's far from out of poems: the one about the hilarious stickball bat he made out of an old broom; the wonderful translation about the death of an ox. Then there is the poem, wonderfully true to the genre of such poems, to a woman remembered, he and the woman as they disappear from the fantasy of invitation:

All shapes will disappear from my mind,
even the ghost of you lingering there,
your voice coming down the stairwell,
"Is that you, Richard?" "It's me."

He's right there and now in these poems.

**David Ferry, author of *Of No Country I Know*
and translator of *The Aeneid***

Richard Fein's poems are gnarly, like root wood. They are anti-perspectival: he keeps his eyes locked in tight focus. The reader's rewards are a sharpened appetite for the particular, an intensified celebration of the textures of the real. The real may be anything for Fein, from clothespins on a line to a nearly worn-out dictionary, to a most touching portrait of the Yiddish poet Yankev Glatshteyn sitting in a poorhouse across from God, who's seated on a bench, worn-out and sick, like a mocked, rejected beggar. And Fein speaks to his ancestors in a way that honors their richness.

Fein's erotic poems, like the others, are immediate, still glistening with sweat. So with his poems about Yiddish, which he loves, and with his poems of old age, so existential that younger readers might want to back away, but they shouldn't, since, if they're lucky, such advanced old age will come to them.

Bert Stern, author of *What I Got for a Dollar*

MUDFISH INDIVIDUAL POET SERIES

Box Turtle Press